# Counting Seeds

Written by Margie Burton,

I am going
to count the seeds.

3

Look at
the big seed.
It is in the avocado.

5

Look at
the little seed.
It is in the pod.

# The pumpkin has seeds.

# The pepper has seeds.

The apple has seeds.

The orange has seeds.

Do you like watermelon?
It has seeds, too!

# Do you like sunflower seeds?

# The birds do!

# He likes seeds, too!